AF604540

When travelling to unknown places
don't forget to pack

a little **courage**,
a little **hope**,
and a little **something special**
to remind you of home.

I hope it's pretty there

ALEX KOPP

ILLUSTRATIONS BY KEVIN VINDEG

Jessie and Joseph wound the music box and the wooden swan on top went round and round to the sound of the tinkling chime.

“What do you think it will be like, this Swan River place?” Joseph asked.

“I don't know,” said Jessie, “but I bet it will be pretty. Or maybe it will be really strange. Maybe the trees will be pink, and scary creatures will come out of them at night and eat you up!”

Joseph giggled. “Well, I think it will be a great adventure.”

Mama was in a tizz. The bed groaned under lumps of clothing. Pa's medical equipment, pots, pans, books, boots, and just about every other household item lay stacked against the walls.

A big wooden chest lay in front of Mama. She put things into it, pulled things out, and then put them in again.

"Oh, what shall I pack?" she cried in dismay.

“We can only take what we need,” Pa said. “There will be no shops where we are going... and there won't be much room on the ship.”

“Does that mean I can't take my music box?” Jessie asked.

Pa shook his head sadly. He carefully cut the swan off the box, and Mama helped Jessie make a pretty lace bag for it. Jessie held it tightly.

“It will always remind me of home,” she said.

On the way to the docks it snowed. It was the sticky sort of snow that melted when it touched the ground, mixed with grime, and turned to grey slush.

Mama took baby Eliza, Jessie, Joseph, and little Henry and Edward for a hot cider. They watched from the inn as Pa supervised men loading their luggage onto *Parmelia*.

Mama looked weary, but Joseph's eyes were wide with awe. "She is beautiful," he said.

"I bet you want to climb the rigging," Jessie teased. Joseph nodded, grinning.

Below deck it was dim and the air was damp and stale.
Men moved crates and barrels into the hold, shouting instructions over each other.

Pa went to meet the captain and Mama struggled with a straw mattress.

The crew weighed anchor by mid afternoon. High above, agile crewmen scurried up the ratlines, unfurling the sails to catch the breeze.

As *Parmelia* slowly moved away, Joseph and Jessie peered over the railing on their tippy toes and waved to the crowd of well-wishers lining the docks.

"Goodbye England! Goodbye!" they called.

As land faded away the sky turned grey and heavy.
Icy wind blew from the north, bringing with it thick raindrops and thunder.

The ship pushed across the open ocean, pitching and rolling
through angry, heaving swell.

"Batten down the hatches!" yelled the ship's first mate.

Down below, the sounds of retching mixed with moans and urgent prayers. Pa, himself pale faced, took up his doctor's bag and made his way to the sick passengers.

Boxes moved and shifted, and Mama's hat case fell down with a thud. Cook put out the galley fires for safety, but no one felt like eating anyway.

Jessie pulled her little swan from its lacy bag.

"I hope it's pretty when we get there," she whispered.

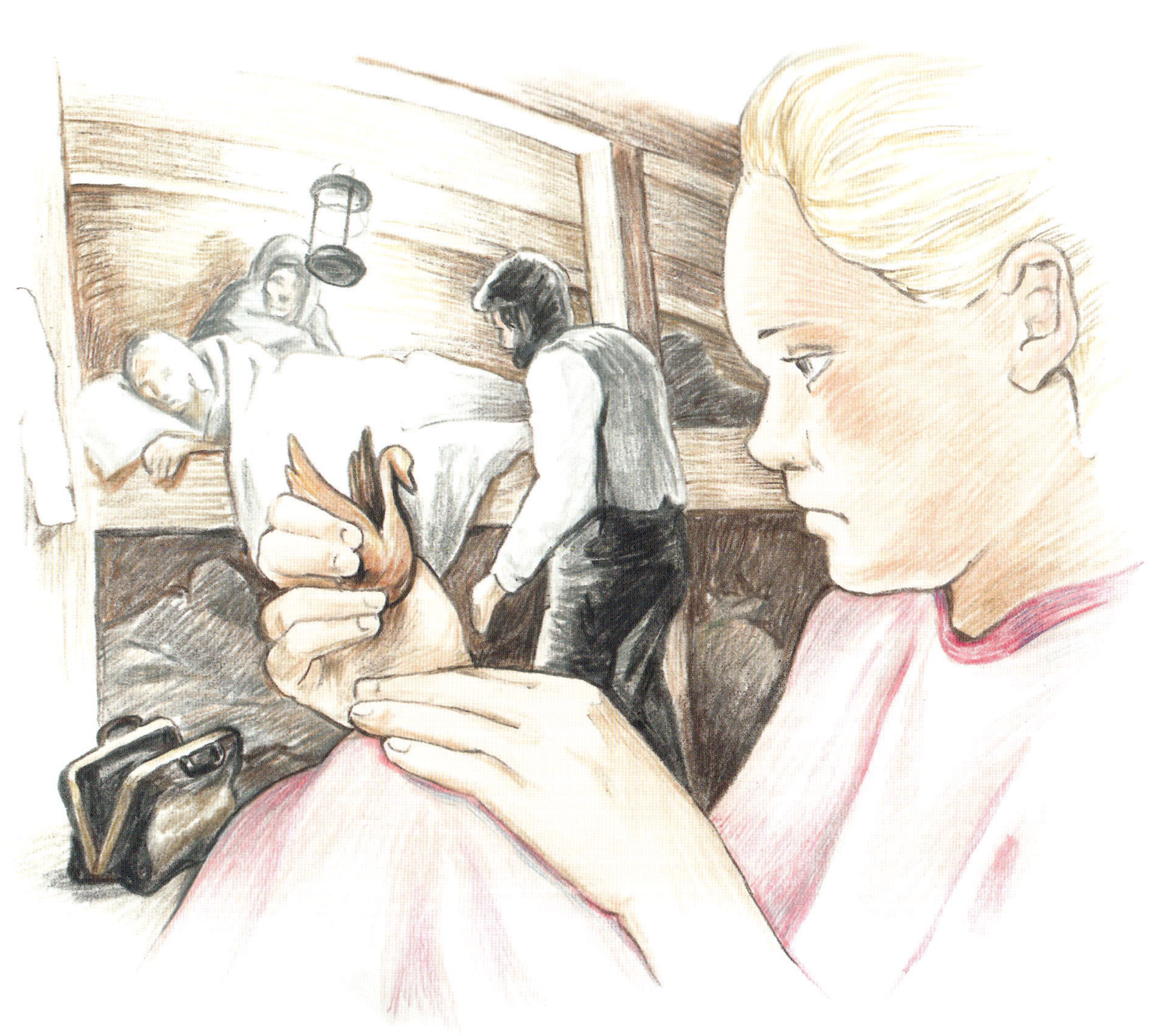

Later, Jessie helped Mama do the washing and they hung it out to dry upon the rigging. Joseph played hide and seek with Edward and Henry, and tried to copy knots he had watched the sailors tie.

The children made new friends on board, and when they spotted another ship on the horizon they scared each other into thinking that it was a pirate ship.

As the days grew hot and humid, food went rotten, water stored in wooden barrels turned a slimy green, and everybody fought for space to sleep on deck. There was always someone in the sick bay, so Pa was kept busy.

There was much excitement when *Parmelia* neared the tip of Africa and entered Table Bay. Men rowed boats towards the coast and returned with fresh supplies.

"Please, Pa," begged Joseph and Jessie, "please may we go on shore, too?"

It was strange to walk on solid ground again after several weeks at sea. Joseph and Jessie skipped along, taking in the sights and smells of the settlement: its dusty streets and dingy alleyways, its gardens and villas, and its crowded shacks.

They bought fresh oranges from a bustling market stall and ate them. The juice dripped down their chins — although Joseph and Jessie didn't notice, for they were too busy looking round at the sailors and soldiers, the sellers and slaves, and the local gentlemen who gathered around them, curious for news from England.

By the time they got back to their boat, storm clouds gathered and it had begun to get dark. The men rowed hard back towards *Parmelia* as the sun dropped beneath the ocean. They heaved and pulled, but made slow progress against the wind and rolling swell.

Suddenly, a huge wave rose high over the boat. Jessie screamed, and Pa reached out for her as the wall of water towered above and crashed onto the boat, washing them into the darkness.

Joseph felt himself being swept into the sea, and grasped for something, anything.
His hand caught a piece of driftwood and he pulled himself up,
gasping for air as his head cleared the surface.

“Pa! Jessie!” he yelled.

But the only reply was the sound of the wild wind,
whistling and squealing around him.

And just like that, his father and sister were gone.

Mama curled on her straw mattress and let darkness absorb her tears. She cuddled the baby closely, but spoke to no one.

Little Henry and Edward wandered the deck, clinging to Joseph as if scared to let him out of their sight, in case he, too, might vanish.

As days turned to weeks, Joseph's favourite part of the ship became the bow, where he could see the world ahead and be alone with his thoughts.

He had found Jessie's swan and he would lay it in his hand, and allow his eyes to scan the horizon in search of land.

"I hope it's pretty there," he heard Jessie say in his head.

"I see it! I see it!"

Suddenly the decks became crowded as all of *Parmelia*'s passengers rushed to have a look at a line of faint sand dunes appearing on the horizon. Even Mama came out.

"I thought there would be mountains," said one.

"I thought it would be greener," said another.

Several small islands lay off the coast.

Parmelia anchored near one of them, for a storm was brewing and the surging gale and rising swell made entry into the sound impossible that night.

Next morning they tried again, wary of jagged rocks and treacherous sand bars that lay hidden under the surface.

Without warning, a dull thud arose from below the water line.
The ship shuddered and jolted, throwing people against each other.

“We've run aground!” shouted the first mate to Captain Stirling.

One by one, the women and children were taken to a tiny island nearby so as to lighten the ship's load.

They took what shelter they could find among the low, rocky outcrops.

Joseph tried to be grown up like Pa and make a fire, but the damp driftwood and howling wind stopped any flames taking hold.

Mama laid out their meagre supply of ship biscuits so that they could soften in the rain.

They huddled together in the cold, looking to the mainland and knowing it was there, yet unable to see it for the cloud.

"I hope it's pretty there,"
thought Joseph,
clutching Jessie's swan.

Finally, *Parmelia* shifted from its sandy platform.

Unable to reach the mainland, she limped towards another, bigger island. As the storm raged, weary travellers climbed ashore.

Joseph trudged over the sandy dunes, carrying as many boxes as he could. He pushed them close together, and Edward and Henry found grass and twigs to stick between the gaps to help keep out the wind.

Mama spread a sheet of canvas over the top and dug little hollows in the ground for them to curl up in for the night.

"Tomorrow, we will make things better," she said.

Slowly, things did become better. Mama cried a little less, the baby grew, and Edward and Henry left Joseph's side. They put up a better tent and some people even started building wooden houses.

They planted seeds and they called the island 'Garden Island'. Soon, more and more ships came, and dropped anchor nearby.

Captain Stirling made his way across the sound,
then further inland and onto the muddy banks of a winding river.

There, he ordered a tree to be cut down,
and said that a big city will stand there one day.

Eventually, Joseph and his family made their way to the river too. By then, it was springtime. The water glistened and sparkled, and warm air blew at their skin.

They saw gently sloping hills, fresh scented trees and bushes of pink, white and yellow flowers.

They looked back towards the river. Suddenly, Mama gasped. "Look!" she said, pointing to a graceful, long-necked bird gliding across the water.

In his pocket, Joseph wrapped his fingers around a little lacy bag with a swan inside it. He thought of Jessie, and Pa, and the slushy snow back home.

"It sure is pretty here," he said.

THE HISTORY BEHIND THE STORY

I hope it's pretty there is based on the true story of the Daly family, who were among the first European settlers to come to the Swan River Colony. Dr Tully Daly was to be the assistant surgeon at the Swan River Colony. He left England aboard *Parmelia* in February 1829, along with his wife Jane, and his five children: Jessie Jane (8), Joseph (6), Henry (4), Edward (2), and 2 month old Eliza Rose.

About half way through the journey, *Parmelia* pulled in at Table Bay, South Africa, to collect supplies. There was a heavy swell when some of the passengers were coming back from a shore visit. As their tender boat reached *Parmelia*, it was swamped by a wave and Dr Daly and his eldest daughter Jessie were washed overboard.

The surviving members of the Daly family carried on to Western Australia. They sighted land at the end of May and dropped anchor near Rottnest Island. However, as *Parmelia* tried to near the shore, it got stuck on a sandbank. To lighten the load, the women and children were quickly moved to nearby Carnac Island, while the men worked to move the ship. Jane Daly and her children would have spent up to five days on Carnac Island, in heavy wind and rain and with no shelter.

Eventually, *Parmelia* was saved and its passengers moved to Garden Island, unloaded stores, set up tents and built brushwood huts. The weather remained very stormy, and it was a few more days before anyone was able to go to the mainland.

It took some time for the Swan River and immediate surrounding area to be explored. The site for the city of Perth was formally announced on the 12th of August, and soldiers' barracks and other buildings started to be built nearby. Since Dr Tully Daly was part of the army, his family was most likely supported by the military and located close to the soldiers' quarters.

It is not clear what happened to Jane, Joseph, Henry, Edward and Eliza Daly. There is record of Jane being seen on a boat heading to Fremantle in January of 1830, and it is believed that she and her children left the colony very soon after, heading for New South Wales or back to England.

THE AUTHOR

Alex got the idea to write about Jessie and Joseph when working at the WA Museum. Being at the Museum was super cool. She got to find out about West Australian history and environment, talk about it with kids and fiddle with all sorts of old stuff. Before that she was a teacher, which was also cool, even though it involved less dress ups and more marking.

Alex grew up in Poland. When she was 10, her parents told her that their family were going to start a new life in another place. They weren't quite sure where that place would be. They went to Austria, then New Zealand, and finally made their way to the shores of the Swan River in Perth. At the time, Alex didn't know what her new home would look like, but remembers hoping that it would be pretty there.

THE ILLUSTRATOR

Kevin also has a great job. He gets to draw pictures and design books, posters, magazines and all sorts of other things, and actually get paid for it. He began drawing at a young age and has had a lifelong interest in art. Since graduating from the Alberta College of Art and Design, he has worked as a designer and illustrator in both Canada and Australia.

Originally from Saskatoon, Canada, he moved to Australia with his wife and two boys and now lives in Perth, Western Australia.

Published 2021 by the
Western Australian Museum
Locked Bag 49, Welshpool DC,
Western Australia 6986
www.museum.wa.gov.au

Illustrations by Kevin Vindeg.
Layout and design by Tim Cumming.
Printed by the Australian Book Connection.

ISBN: 978-1-925040-35-7 (hardcover)
A catalogue record for this book is available from the National Library of Australia.

The Western Australian Museum acknowledges and respects the Traditional Owners of their ancestral lands, waters and skies.